The Big Golden Book of
BOATS AND SHIPS

By Patricia Relf
Illustrated by Tom LaPadula

A GOLDEN BOOK • NEW YORK
Western Publishing Company, Inc., Racine, Wisconsin 53404

Acknowledgments

Many thanks to the sailors and others who patiently answered
my questions for this book, especially:

Captain Richard Allen, Atlantic Offshore Fishermen's Association;
Captain Richard Cullison, Sandy Hook Pilots; Norwegian Lines;
Dr. Lewis Strong; U.S. Coast Guard; U.S. Navy

For Wm, Louise, and Emily
—*P.R.*

In Memory of John
—*T.L.*

Contents

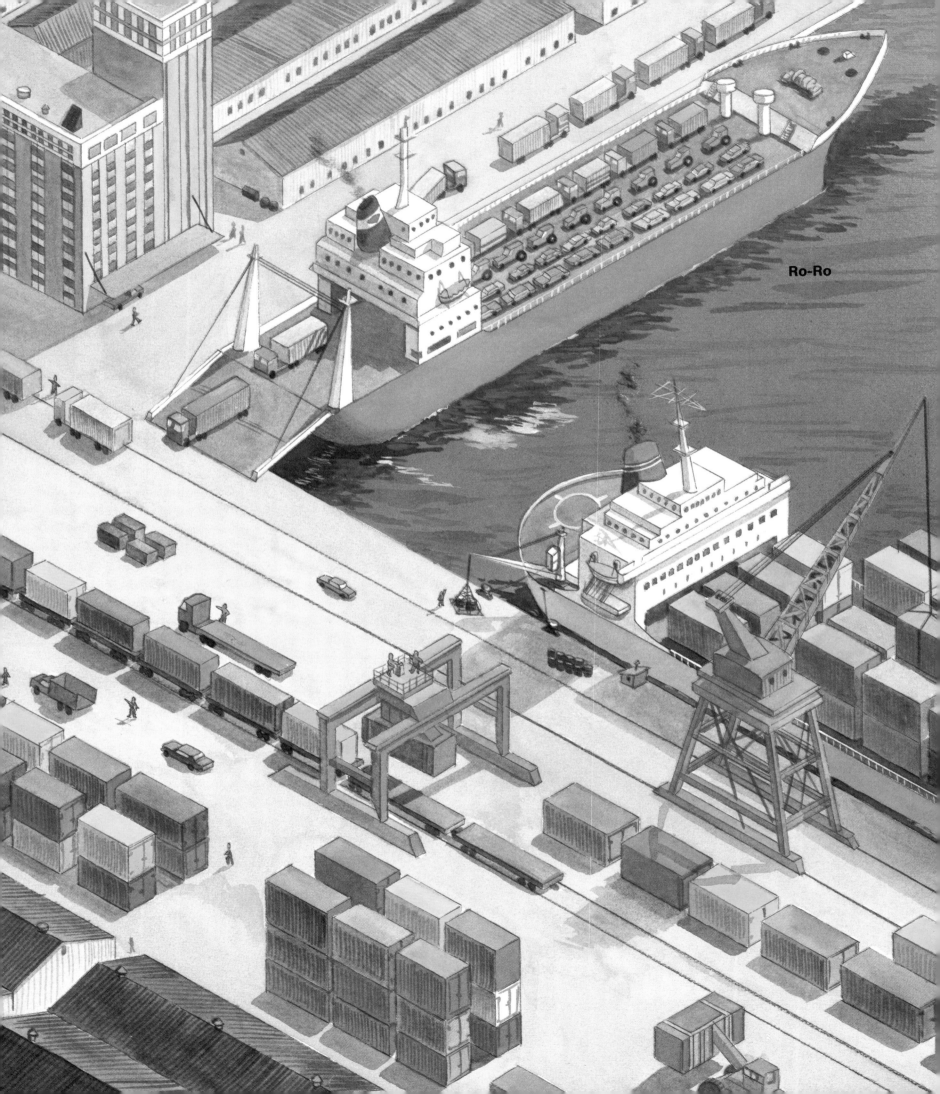

Ro-Ro

The World of Boats

A busy port is a good place to see different kinds of boats and ships. At a large port, workers load and unload cargo ships from all over the world. Special cranes are used to lift huge boxes, called containers, off a ship's deck or out of its hold. Straddle carriers then put the containers onto flatbed trucks or train cars that will take them to their next destination.

New automobiles, trucks, and tractors are driven off a ship called a Ro-Ro, which is short for Roll-on, Roll-off. A Ro-Ro carries its own ramp and needs no special equipment at a dock for loading and unloading.

Big cargo ships are difficult to steer into a crowded, busy harbor, so powerful tugboats are used to guide them to and from the dock.

What is the difference between a boat and a ship? A boat is smaller than a ship—usually operated by just a few people.

cargo ship

tugboats

9

mainmast

mizzenmast

poop deck

foremast

bowsprit

Ships With Sails

More than four hundred years ago, this English galleon was the fastest merchant ship and the finest fighting ship to sail on any sea. It could fire seventeen-pound cannonballs at targets over two thousand feet away, the length of seven football fields.

Thousands of years before sailing ships such as this were launched, sails had already been invented as a way to harness the wind. Ancient Egyptians designed and built sailboats over five thousand years ago.

11

Chinese junks have been used for hundreds of years to carry all kinds of goods, from rice to gold. A junk has a flat bottom and one to five large, square sails. The sails are made of woven mats. Bamboo crosspieces keep the sails stiff.

Sails are not used on barges—long, flat boats built to carry freight. Today, many barges move under their own motor power. One hundred and fifty years ago, in the busy days of the Erie Canal, horses and mules pulled barges up and down the canal.

When clipper ships were first built more than one
hundred years ago, they raced through water faster
than any ship before them. Thanks to their long,
pointed hulls and many sails, they cut standard
shipping times in half. By the early 1900's,
the majestic clippers were replaced by
steam-powered ships.

The Steamboat Is Coming

A century ago, elegant steamboats carried passengers up
and down the Mississippi and other American rivers. At first
the steamboats used wood as fuel. A woodburning furnace
boiled water to make steam, which turned the paddle wheels.
Later steamboats used coal as fuel. Riding on a riverboat was a
lively adventure. Boilers sometimes exploded, and the
riverboats often ran aground.

Why Do Boats Float?

Many objects float in water—but why? If you push down on a beach ball that is floating in water, you can feel the water pressing back and pushing the ball up against your hands. The water that the beach ball has pushed aside, or displaced, is pressing back against the ball. This pressure is called buoyancy. Buoyancy is the force that makes the ball float.

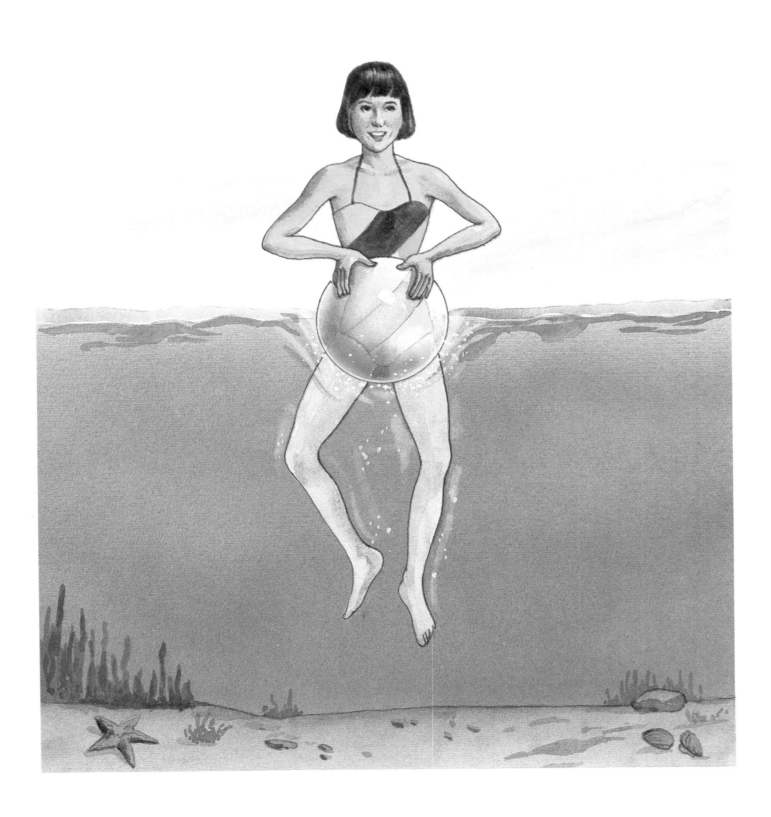

The beach ball is full of air, so it is very light. It weighs less than the water it displaces. But if you filled the beach ball with sand, it would be heavier than the water it displaced. An object that is heavier than water sinks.

It would seem that a huge ship with a hull made of steel would sink, too. But the ship is hollow. Inside it is filled with air. Water is heavy. The weight of the steel and air together is still less than the weight of the water that the ship displaces. Since the whole ship weighs less than water, it floats.

Boats to the Rescue

Coast Guard boats are used to patrol the shoreline, search for missing ships, and rescue disabled ships and crews. They also help enforce fishing laws and stop people from smuggling drugs and other illegal goods into the country. Like police cars, Coast Guard boats have loud sirens and high-powered searchlights.

Large Coast Guard vessels are called cutters. The largest ones have flight decks for helicopter takeoffs and landings. Small Coast Guard vessels are used as chase or rescue boats.

The powerful pumps on a fireboat shoot heavy sprays of water onto burning ships or docks. Fireboats can be found in every large port in the world. Some of these boats sail out of port to help ships that are far out at sea.

An accident on an oil tanker may cause oil to spill into a lake or ocean. To keep the oil from spreading, two boats tow a long, flexible boom, or line of floats, around the oil spill. Then a skimmer sucks the oil from the surface of the water.

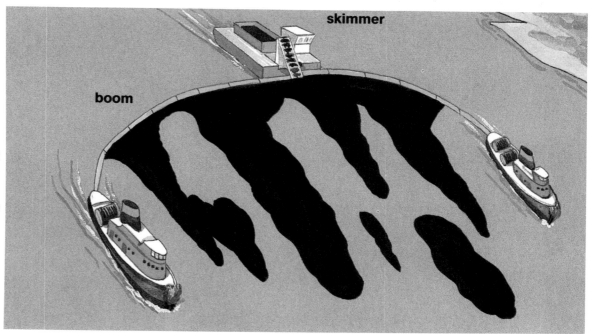

A powerful oceangoing tugboat rushes to help when a ship at sea gets into trouble. If an abandoned ship is saved and towed to port, the tugboat owner is paid a high fee for the salvage, or rescue, work.

Submersibles are small submarines used for research or salvage work. They can dive far deeper than human scuba divers.

In 1986, a submersible called *Alvin* finally reached the wreck of the *Titanic,* a luxury passenger liner that struck an iceberg in the North Atlantic and sank in 1912. The three scientists inside *Alvin* sent a small swimming robot inside the *Titanic.* The robot, attached to *Alvin* by a long cable, carried a camera and sent back live pictures as it traveled through the ghostly staterooms of the sunken liner.

Submersibles have been used since the 1960's to do scientific research. They have mechanical claws for picking things up, traps for capturing sea creatures, and corers for taking samples of mud, sand, and rocks. A submersible once helped to recover a bomb lost in water half a mile deep.

When There Is Ice

Icebreakers clear passages through frozen waters so that other ships can sail through. The icebreaker's powerful engines push the bow, or front of the ship, up on top of the ice. The weight of the ship then presses down on the ice to break it into pieces.

The bow and sides of the ship are armored for extra strength. Propellers at the front and back of an icebreaker help the ship move easily in either direction. Some Arctic icebreakers can break up ice that is thirty feet thick—the height of a three-story house!

The Biggest Ships

Supertankers are the largest ships in the world. These gigantic vessels carry oil from the Middle East, Africa, and South America. This one is more than a quarter of a mile long and weighs more than six hundred thousand tons, fully loaded. That is almost twice as heavy as the Empire State Building!

The hull of a supertanker is divided into many separate compartments so that huge amounts of oil cannot slosh from side to side and capsize the ship.

To avoid scraping the ocean floor, this supertanker needs to float in water that is more than eighty-one feet deep. That means she can only tie up at deepwater ports. If a harbor is shallow, the tanker anchors at sea and either pumps its oil into a smaller tanker or into hoses leading to an underwater pipeline.

Lighting the Way

Lighthouses have been used for thousands of years to warn ships not to sail too close to dangerous rocks or shallow water. The bright lights of some lighthouses can be seen forty nautical miles away. In the past, lighthouse keepers lived in the lighthouses all year round to keep the machinery working. Now most lighthouses work automatically and need little care.

In waters where lighthouses could not be built, lightships showed sailors the way. Crews lived aboard the lightships. Even the toughest sailors sometimes grew seasick on these ships, since they were always moored—tied up or anchored—in the roughest waters.

Today, most lightships have been replaced by buoys or light platforms on tall stilts, called Texas towers.

Signal Flags and Lights

The most important signal flag a ship flies is its ensign, showing country of origin. Other kinds of signal flags make it possible to spell out messages, letter by letter. Warships often use signal flags, and cargo ships sometimes use them, too. A full set of signal flags includes one flag for each letter of the alphabet, one flag for each number (zero through nine), three triangular flags that indicate when letters are repeated, plus a flag that means a message has been understood.

To avoid collisions at night, ships and boats show signal lights. Red and green lights mean that a vessel is moving. Green is used on the starboard, or right, side. Red is used on the port, or left, side. At anchor, a boat uses only white lights. A small vessel uses just one white light, while a large vessel shows two. The bow, or front, light is always higher than the stern, or back, light.

Which Direction?

When sailors are out of sight of land, they see nothing but water. How do sailors know where they are? How do they reach their destination? Using nautical maps and instruments to find your way at sea is called navigation.

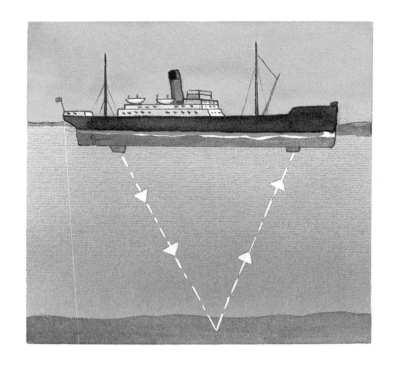

Finding out how deep the water is helps sailors to figure out how close they are to land. Today, many ships use sonar equipment to measure water depth. A sonar transmitter sends sound waves down into the water. The time it takes the sound waves to travel to the ocean bottom and bounce back to the ship tells the sonar operator how deep the water is. Sonar stands for SOund Navigation And Ranging.

Sailors have always used the sun and stars to guide them. The sun rises in the east. Heading toward the sun in the morning, sailors know that they are sailing east.

A sextant can measure the height of the sun in the sky. If navigators know the height of the sun, they can also figure out mathematically how far north or south they are from the equator—the imaginary line around the fattest part of the earth. To measure the height of the sun, a navigator looks at the horizon through the eyepiece of a sextant and moves the index arm until the mirror at the end of it reflects the sun next to the horizon.

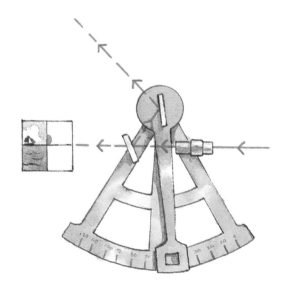

For many centuries, it was difficult for a ship to figure out its position at night or in bad weather. Today, many boats are equipped with radio direction finders. The receiver on a boat picks up radio signals from special transmitters called beacons. The source of the beacon may be in a tower on land or in a buoy. The sailor turns the boat's antenna until the beacon signal is strongest. A compass then shows the sailor the direction of the beacon.

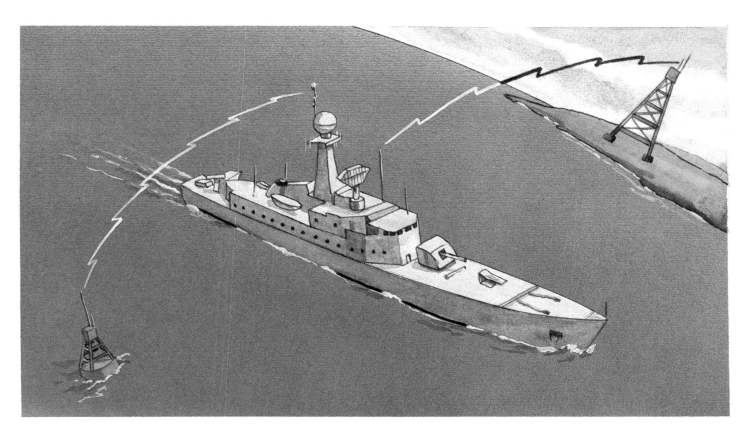

Satellite signals pinpoint a ship's position very accurately. A ship that can receive a signal from a satellite can compute the ship's exact position at sea to within fifty feet.

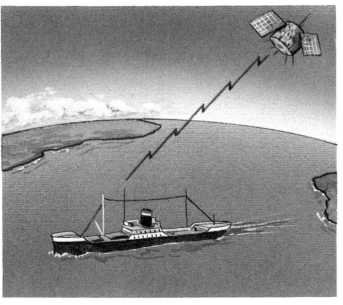

An Airport at Sea

An aircraft carrier is a floating naval airport that can travel wherever it's needed.

A carrier's flight deck may look long, but in fact it is much shorter than an ordinary runway. Jet aircraft aboard carriers need help to take off and land in such small spaces. During takeoff, a hook pulls the plane along the deck at a very fast speed and then shoots it off the carrier like a giant slingshot.

Landing a jet on the deck of a moving ship is difficult. In order to fly in at just the right angle, the jet pilot must listen carefully to radio commands from the air control tower, called the "island." To help the plane stop before it dives off the end of the ship, the carrier has four big cables stretched across its flight deck. A hook on the tail of the plane catches one of the cables. With a loud screech and a sudden jerk, the plane is brought to a stop.

After the jet has landed, a tractor tows it to its parking spot. Later, an elevator takes the plane below to the hangar deck for maintenance.

Silent Submarines

A nuclear-powered attack submarine like this one travels underwater very quietly and can patrol the oceans without being seen or heard by enemy ships or airplanes.

How does a submarine dive and surface?

Like an empty jar, a submarine floats when it is full of air. Empty, it weighs less than the water it displaces. But if the crew lets water in to fill up the large empty spaces called ballast tanks, the submarine sinks into the water.

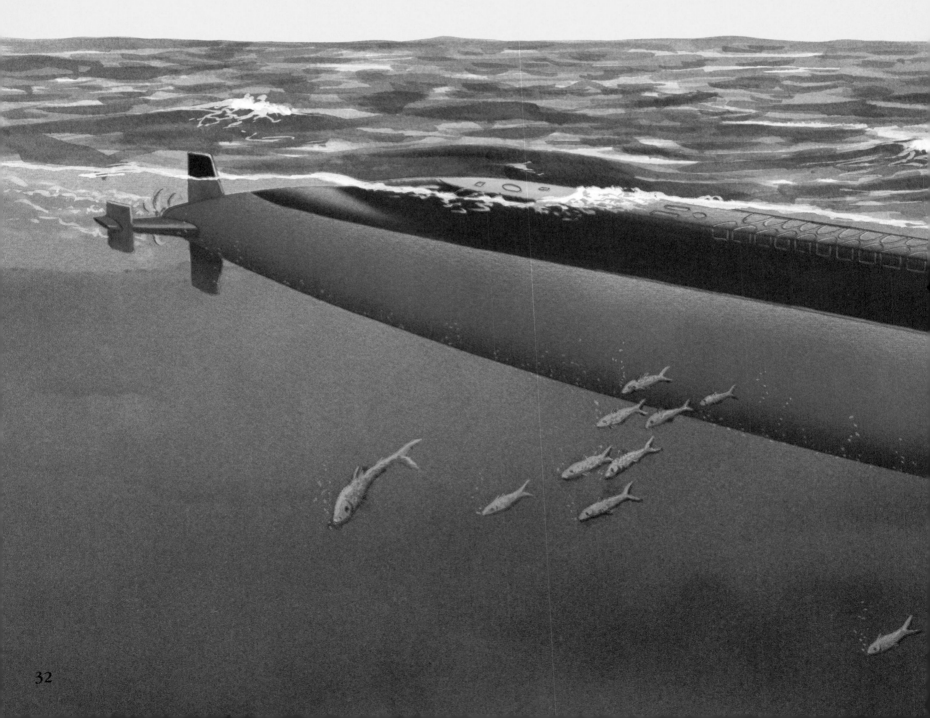

The submarine with water added weighs more than the displaced water alone. To surface, the crew uses a blast of air to push the water out of the ballast tanks.

When the submarine is close to the surface, officers can see what is up at the top by looking through the periscope in the submarine's control room.

City at Sea

A luxury liner is like a floating city. On a large liner, there can be as many as two thousand passengers, who can eat, shop, go dancing, see movies, get their hair cut, or go for a dip in one of the ship's swimming pools. Each night a different group of passengers is invited to dine at the captain's table.

The ship's cabins are just like hotel rooms, with comfortable berths, or beds, television sets, and private bathrooms. Passengers can call anywhere in the world from telephones in their cabins.

Meet the Officers and Crew

Who does what on board a ship? Here are some of the important officers and members of the crew.

captain

1. The captain, or skipper, is in charge of the entire ship and makes the major decisions about the ship's course and schedule. At sea, his or her word is law.

first mate

2. The first mate is the captain's assistant. He or she supervises the day-to-day work on the ship and manages the crew.

chief engineer

3. The chief engineer is in charge of running and repairing the ship's engines and other machinery.

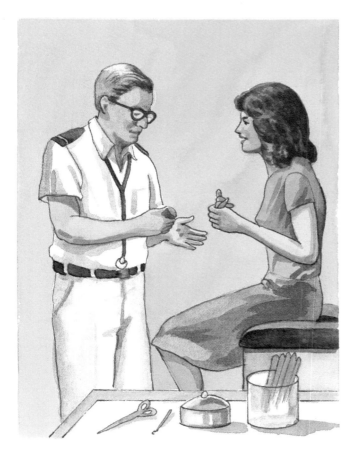

4. The ship's doctor takes care of any sick passengers and crew members.

5. The chef cooks and supervises workers in the kitchen, or galley.

6. The chief radio operator handles ship-to-shore and ship-to-ship communications.

7. The cruise director organizes activities and entertainment for passengers.

spinnaker

Sailboats of Today

Modern sailboats can be very simple or very complicated, like the yachts built in various countries to compete in the famous America's Cup race. To design the fastest possible sailboat for the race, as much as fifteen million dollars may be spent on a single boat. Sophisticated computers on board such a boat help the captain make lightning-fast decisions.

A simpler sailboat can be used for a regatta, or race, or just for an afternoon sail. Most boats use a large mainsail and a smaller jib. For extra speed, a big, colorful spinnaker is hoisted.

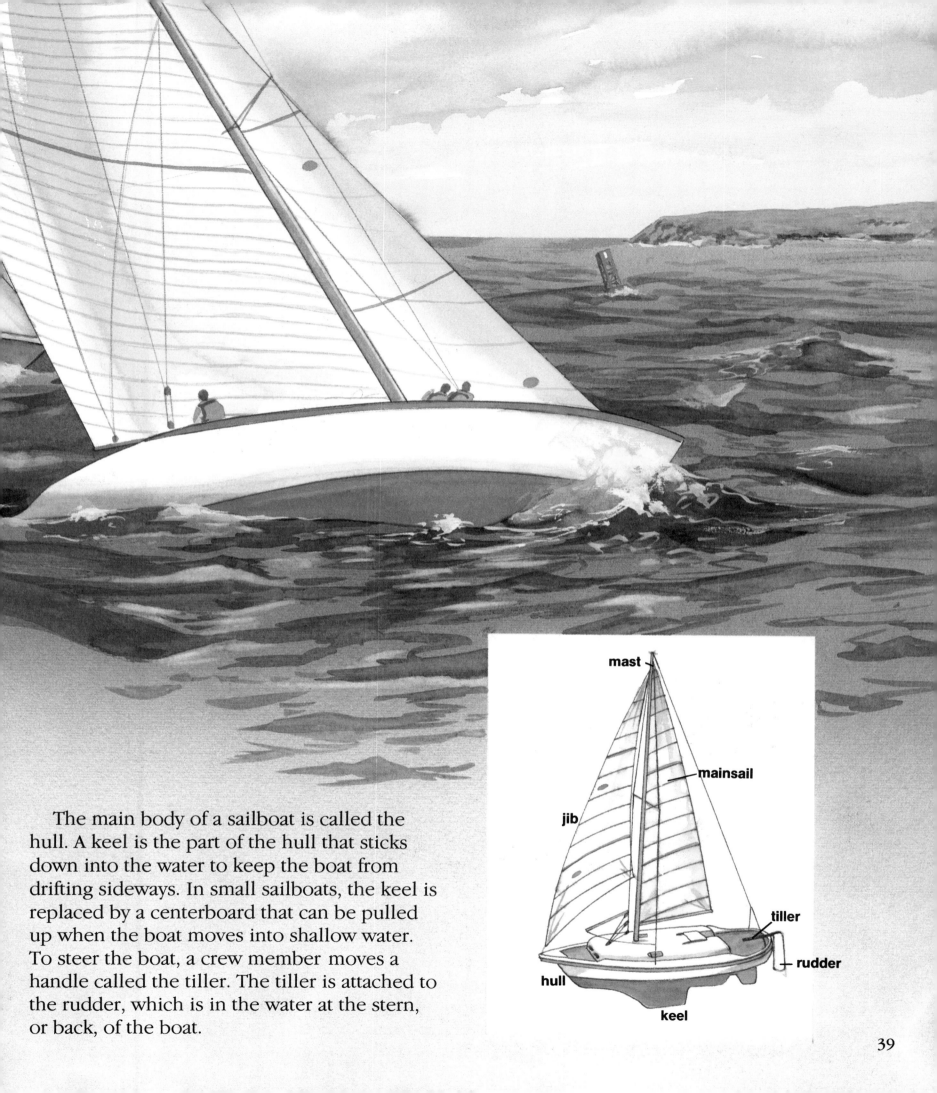

The main body of a sailboat is called the hull. A keel is the part of the hull that sticks down into the water to keep the boat from drifting sideways. In small sailboats, the keel is replaced by a centerboard that can be pulled up when the boat moves into shallow water. To steer the boat, a crew member moves a handle called the tiller. The tiller is attached to the rudder, which is in the water at the stern, or back, of the boat.

mast

mainsail

jib

tiller

rudder

hull

keel

speedboat

Motorboats

Motorboat is a name given to a boat driven by any kind of engine except a steam engine. These boats can be simple or fancy—from a small outboard motorboat to a powerful speedboat or large yacht.

yacht

outboard motorboat

Hovercraft

A Hovercraft, or air-cushion vehicle, rides above the water's surface on a pillow of air. Some Hovercraft are amphibious. In other words, they can travel on water or land.

How does a Hovercraft work? A large fan pushes air down against the water or ground under the craft. The air pressure then lifts the Hovercraft so that it sits on a layer of air. On many Hovercraft, a flexible skirt on the bottom of the vessel helps keep air from escaping.

fan

42

Hydrofoils

At slow speeds, a hydrofoil looks like an ordinary boat. But a hydrofoil has large foils, like wings, attached to its hull, or body. When the craft begins to go fast, its hull lifts up. Water moving over the foils pushes the boat up out of the water.

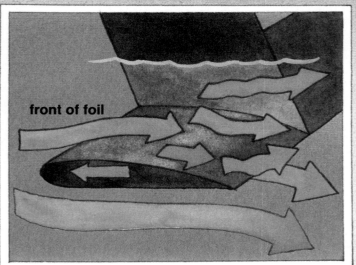

front of foil

Jetboats

A jetboat is very speedy. It has no propeller beneath the hull. Instead, the hull sucks in water and forces it back out through a nozzle at the stern. The powerful jet of water pushes the boat forward.

Once this fast boat is skimming along, it can travel over water that is only four inches deep. A jetboat can also make a U-turn almost instantly—in the space of just one boat length.

Nautical Terms

aft: toward the stern, or back, of a boat or ship

anchor: a heavy object lowered on a strong line or chain to the floor of a lake or ocean that holds a ship in place

ballast: heavy material used to weigh a vessel down

bow: the front end of a ship

buoy: a float that is anchored in position to mark a waterway or something underwater

buoyancy: the tendency to float in water

cabin: a room on a ship

capsize: to turn over accidentally in a boat

cargo: goods or freight carried by a ship

compass: an instrument used to determine direction, usually with a magnetic needle that points to the north

crew: a group of people working on a boat

deck: a flat surface on a boat similar to the floor of a building

ensign: the national flag flown by a ship

fore: toward the bow, or front, of a boat

galley: a ship's kitchen; also, a large, ancient ship powered by oars

hatch: an opening in the deck of a ship that lets people or cargo pass in and out of the hull

head: the toilet on a boat

hold: the inside of a ship, especially the space used for cargo

hull: the main body of a ship or boat; the part that floats in the water

jib: a triangular sail on the front of a sailboat

knot: one nautical mile; or a speed of one nautical mile per hour

line: a length of rope

mast: an upright pole that holds a sail and any ropes and other poles used to control it; a foremast is a front mast; the mainmast is the tallest; a mizzenmast is an aft mast

nautical mile: a distance on water of 6,076 feet

periscope: a tube containing lenses and mirrors that lets a person see over or around things; found on submarines

port: the left side of a ship or boat, as seen by someone facing forward on the vessel; also, a harbor or area of calm water for ships and boats to load and unload cargo

propeller: a kind of wheel with twisted blades that spin to move a boat through water

rigging: the sails, attached lines, and masts of a sailboat

rudder: a flat board or piece of metal attached to the stern, or back, of a boat and used for steering

sail: a piece of fabric, such as canvas, set out so that the wind can push against it to move a boat through water

sonar: a system using sound waves for locating underwater objects; sonar stands for SOund Navigation And Ranging

spinnaker: a large, triangular sail used on a sailboat for extra speed

starboard: the right side of a ship or boat, as seen by someone facing forward on the vessel

stern: the back end of a ship or boat

tiller: a lever attached to a rudder, used to steer a boat